ALIAS CITY

Carol Frost

MADHAT PRESS
CHESHIRE, MASSACHUSETTS

MadHat Press
PO Box 422, Cheshire MA 01225

The Library of Congress has assigned
this edition a Control Number of
2019954698

ISBN 978-1-941196-95-3 (paperback)

Cover design by Marc Vincenz
Cover image adapted from *NE Street in Cairo*
by Konstantin Yegorovich Makovsky (1839–1915)
Author photo by Mark Terry
Book design by MadHat Press

www.MadHat-Press.com

for
Luca, Marco, and Zoë

and in memoriam
Renée Fellner

TABLE OF CONTENTS

Evening light rushing back, back rushing away—what I felt at
what I saw

in return to Stephansdom—
heart's sweet wren and roar—
and by lindens every spring.

The mind goes, and the past
fits itself around the ankles
of what may have been.

—RF

City with First-Class Funerals

Angels are coming on vacation to our city—with the funeral
a wine feast, a beautiful corpse in brooch light,
mourners, their cathedral calm.
Er hat den 71er gekommen, the joke goes,
and all here can remember sweet spring chaos,
succulences in summer, the good fall like a woman
lying nakedly on a pelt,
and from north windows, years inevitably brought to their knees
like someone's son executed by a river.
The service is ending,
the representatives of the Union of Cemetery Singers have left
by the back door, and I think Omama, grown suspicious of
          strangers,
more appreciates the candelabras, lilies, red, red carnations,
and chrysanthemums festooning the caisson carrying her
to the family tomb. Her triumph was to be the reason
for all these flowers and the candles,
dark yellow and guttering, as if the wind was testing the
          certainties
to orient her in the grave an east wind.
What of her trysts and pricking conscience,
wrapped away in the godawful mantilla?
Need we speak of them now?
Hush, the souls in the Friedhof der Namenlosen
are whispering, trees in the urn grove rustle, an accordion starts,
he plays like an angel, and it all gets muddled.
Have we given coins to the undertaker?
The caskets are stacked? Then finally

Rudolph is where he wanted to lie, between Omama's mother
and Omama. The rains commence. Let the world
deride or pity. We hear you calling, Lord of wind and flame.

City of the Ridiculous

Ridiculous, we. All the long, bright days. Days
without death. Without without, the without. The suicide leap
    comic as sex—
hips and asses, sweat, rush.
All our acts become gestures of our acts. The litter of the years
has been, swept into another precinct.
A few steps ahead of us, death. And we are left
to ourselves without the means. To revenge,
to throw our bodies at ourselves. Be the voice
of besieging sorrow, we cannot.
Be the wintry sound as of cold spirals
of wind in empty lots, by which those given
a cot and a bowl of greasy soup feel blessed.
It's not in us. A cry of art? Rid of ridiculous us.
The very air is rid of air. We play videos endlessly.
We daydream death in a forest, on a cliff
over the Sea of Japan. In Madrid, Alcalá, 237—
the matador's gaiety and elegance in nearness
to the massive head, the natural beast, death.
In a suit of lights, with wanton thrusts
of hips, he fans death with a gory cape,
wrapped in fire, darkest, pivoting, fire,
at the last second or the second
honor's snuffed, ethos stilled, and death lives.

Brandenburg Gate

Wind slams and opens
the gate, light beating
its bronze horses, heavy-withered.

And Napoleon and Friedrich
belong to the bronze chariot.

And Max Liebermann, and Martha Liebermann
who chose suicide over Theresienstadt
from her apartment in the shadow of entrance

and departure, they are in the bronze horses
that gallop on and on

that all should have their place
rain darkened, star broken.

Dog City

We have seen you following the scent—
heads like shovels, eyes stones,
and then heard you *grrrrrrr*
over the body, bedded then in an alley
or low corner. No reluctance in her young desire,
you say when yousay, yousay
You like it like this, don't you? You like it!
We remember the craven air,
semen on clothes, skin, and dirt,
more so in our city, with its avenues,
high windows, courts, symphony halls.
The child is in darkness,
and we have gone into the cellar
where it is kept. For the sake of a return
to its happiness, how much happiness
would have to be leashed?
We go home with the paradox
that for the city to be what we think
and to live there,
some must be beaten, some raped.
We must know it
as we know Leda and Zeus, Philomena,
Procne, and the King of Thrace.
Dogs are in the streets in suits;
they run loose.

Circus City

This is what life is really like.
This is what life is really like.
This is what life is really like every day.
—Gray Parrot, Vienna, 1943

In the circus animals' diary: "And all this was destroyed in
    ninety minutes."
Makeshift forests flaming to high heavens, metal bent bars.
Siberian tigers, black panthers, jaguars, pumas,
bears, hyenas and wolves, and all the lion pit saved from burning
by the keepers' own hands. By bullets. Only so much can be
    said.
Herbage will be scarce. Nature will gather like sleeping poppies
over the craters and lost species.
The African wart-hog will be cooked over an open fire in the
    garden.
One thinks of one's restlessness, Faustian—
in the minutes-before-dawn dark
with the devil cry of black crows, the miry skull
of the half-eaten rabbit, then gold grimy hills
and light making jewels and hand mirrors among the trees.
Why are you here? It dawns. All this will never be again.
The circus can't be locked.

After I saw my friends dead on the train, I was sent away from the city. My brothers were in the war, my parents still at the apartment on Quellenstrasse. The mountains stirred me, bone cold mist in meadows, and paths that could lead me where everything behind me was forever unfamiliar, unrelated.

Gradually the war came to its close. I saw the mothers of soldiers finding then losing in a crowd their still-journeying sons. The guardian spirits of the road kept dreaming them back. When I decided to leave for good, I smuggled fur coats to earn money for the trip, shadows passing in the cleared fields like boxes of sorrows on either side of the border.

The sky doesn't know
those who died on the road
what they were used to.

—RF

Impressions of the City at Sunrise

Streak of yellow oblong of pink
riff of aluminum red in river
vertical blues and grays
and barges that may as well have set out
from kingdom come in haze
now baskets of red and yellow flowers
with candles in the river eddies
now molten now
yellow stumbling onto wharves
onto the street
while one transit officer ducks into the dark
and knell of a subway staircase
while another is lit through by day
more and more perilous
as if time plotted
bargained new coins minted
morning peering in
at the solitary and unaware
then in sudden vowel
a flame a cry a tableau
early morning in bedclothes
nothing of the night before
centuries couldn't guess
or be tempted by or long after
after it has gone away.

~

Streak of yellow oblong of pink
riff of steel and barges that may as well have set out

from kingdom come in haze
and with candles in the river eddies now yellow stumbling
            onto wharves

onto the street
while one transit officer ducks the dark

and knell of a subway staircase
and another is lit through by day

more and more perilous
tons of light in windows morning coughing in

morning in bedclothes
and night as if ever here but not or too far past

for tantrum
no hands ours anyone's nothing

to stop what's soon and gone

from kingdom come's haze
pink barge riff of steel

tons of light in windows
tantrum with mirrors stories high

facing higher legions
lances, triremes, sails!

City with Rabbit and Crow

First she's thinking about the music museum
in Prague, the period instruments, the period recordings,
then she is remembering the rabbit and the crow
battling last week on the front lawn of her countryside home,
rabbit reeling under the black wings.
What had the crow to do with the spring morning? Or the
        fortepiano
in the museum Mozart once played for the few
in 1847 who came to listen to him? She waved her arms
and saw another crow fly into the deranged light,
something limp in its beak. The rabbit ran, too,
but in days to come sat among those same thorns and cups,
still as a stool in a room full of stools.
She stands behind a window wondering how long
before the rabbit will go for good, no trace left,
no fur scraps, no black feathers. The museum musicians
are gone and their children are gone
and great wars have also passed by.
She doesn't believe grief mattered one way or another.
Once when I was a girl, poison ivy bloated
my face so, my mother let me stay
home from school. Not really ill, I was free to roam
alone in the far fields, and very early that morning
the sound of wind gathering little by little,
elusively, frightened me. Little did I know
what labyrinths living contained, that no matter
how still I kept I already walked there.

Butterfly in the City

Butterfly, no doubt you live within yourself, lifting your veined
    wings,
sipping dirt and nectar from the last geranium on the window
    ledge.

The steep, sooted wind is nothing to think over,
and what of the stone mannerism of mountains on panes of
    city glass—

sun skittering across, now that autumn's come, with its memory
    of fields
where the musk of flowers permeates light itself?

If I have never smelled the smell, I have seen you waft inland
where summers stand in circles of colored air you magnified
    and on currents

seaward from hills where snow had fallen. Yet you are here,
enough gray-pink lighting from shadows for you to live and
    die in,
Butterfly, settled on the sill, drinking in new nature, being.

City Harbor

How often we come to a headland and a city opens,
as when mid-region stars in the Milky Way cast shadows,
and the Great Rift appears—
                    migration, a swarm, an exceeding leap.

Where dogmen rode the crane hook into the air,
and summer's linseed oil blew over the water,
we follow—dreams our nerve tonic where nerve is needed.

The bowl will be broken at the fountain,
The doors will be shut in the streets.
The keepers of the houses will tremble.

But something before we know it is here,
makes us go on, even with mists rising,

to sit in the shade of some trees,
thinking, perhaps, that this finally is the last
of Earth. To be perplexed, but say nothing of it

to the rest. To feel a little light on the skin,
light that enlarges everything
and then lets us alone.

*I'd loved the ones I left in Wien, memory told me. Memory said,
you haven't the right....*

*Exhausted, I fell asleep thinking of the myth of the mantis who
in its exhaustion was laid on a floating flower. In its thigh a seed
was left, all people came to life and nothing yet themselves asked,
"Why am I here," and answered them, "To see what comes."*

*Years collect each night
from low and high and fling them
like darts at a child.*

—RF

Rumored City

Those who travel to this city hear long before
arriving the murmurs as of insects
in the wind that piles up the shadows
and moves the mornings into day.
Such curious stories, half-told,
reach them in winding sunlight,
float as on the surface of a lake trout rise to.

Is this what it is to be caught, to
have suspected not everything in the light
of day was genuine, nothing truly foretold,
but so badly to have wanted the day
and all one's hours lifted from shadow
and seen the feathered, bright insects
darting on the surface and leapt before

thinking? They were untroubled before
the rumor of the darting insect
held in the corner of their mouths. Shadows
bred, ugliness grew, they felt the day
slip into darkness. The story they'd been told
was a trap, light not sunlight,
after all, no place left to travel to.

Mole People

Leeches, slugs, flatworms, beetles, centipedes,
feral cats and dogs, and the cold flames
mole people in city tunnels awaken to.
Ignis fatus, luces del tesoro,
the stories tell, and who isn't a scavenger
of stories? For some the moles are lost
souls, for others hell's embers help
find their bearings. Below squander,
mole people make their lives, receding as night
recedes, advancing in pitch-black
along the lost stream beds, climbing the grates
and into metal dumpsters where
every necessity can be carried underground.
One moleman found a bookcase;
yet, I wonder if I were inside his head,
would I be reading as the moleman or as me?
The sensitivity of my hand
is six times poorer than the star
of the star-nosed mole, and to imagine
its tactile world, all my perception
must be as if my body were all finger and tongue.
But I have little desire to leave
the colorful and airy streets
and cannot imagine myself touching
an arm of the man whose coat is inside out.
The lights in the marshes, it is said,
will follow you but stand still if you stand.

City Pigeons

If the thoughtful naiad by the fountain had more brains
than the children splashing
to say what truly matters, thank god she's held her tongue,

day as ever switching sounds and textures
without bothering to maintain the tempo.

Beware car music the sonic equivalent of interrogation lights.
Beware museums, nature morte, bronze horses charging
endlessly from stone pedestals.

The chuckling animation on ledges, beware; blue pigeons
rebuilding their nests with stems, straws,
shit, the mummies of dead nestlings.

There's not one capable of lying or that knows what death is;
pigeons, too, are responsible for our emotional exhaustion.

Carol Frost

A Good Night's Sleep

Reassured that we return as before, we enter
a land where everything changes, densities, colors,
rhythms of breathing, and we meet the dead.

What sort of name might turn up inside our pockets
if we remained there? The hair stands on end.
The repose around the eyes can't wash off;
it only becomes a little cleaner.

And the ones we did not know we loved
we follow down the nights
in cities half-built of where we've been, half-
        built of ribbons.

… the body itself divine and absent, the lineaments
of beauty stored even more powerfully in thought:
the ankle's pale butterfly in a chrysalis.

What would we know of this going-hence
but the occasional fissure of light?

Ai, the divine ignorance of closed eyes.

… missing only that moment of coming to,
as if giant hands extracted from a small rip in fate and placed
        you,
who counted for so little when liberated in sleep, where you
        last stood.

22

Alias City

They were travelers, plotting river courses,
writing the Genesis of unknown people,
fugitives with a revolver in one hand, reins in another,
merchants among the olive trees, euphorbias, mimosas,
emissaries, deserters. Some knew the native tongues;
they called themselves by new names
in the eastern twilight, different parts of their soul
never having learned to live together.
Skies burned. Dust covered the palms
and minarets as they arrived by the incandescent shore
of our city, each with his own little dreams and disasters.
Some remained, never to be heard of again.
Some left with caravans, wearing native dress—ephemerids.
Where are they? What are they used to?
The only preserved interview—of an artist and explorer.
    Did he ever speak of his friends in X?
    Never. The only thing he liked in X was his sister.
    But did you know that he painted?
    Oh yes!—some fine things: stemware,
    a series of watercolors of shoebills and Abdim's
            stork.

A glimmer sometimes forms as a city forms on the horizon, rivers alongside, lights, lights of cities half-remembered, half never-were. Couldn't I step ashore to a place with its own name and return, knowing the difference between there and here? Was my mind ever mine to have, was my mind given?

Amber-honey cold
mornings humbled by evenings
still I am alive.

—RF

City Near Paradise

1.

Long before you turned on the light, I heard hurricane fill the
    oak.

As morning flowers from hell, little hellish flames,

we are still here. Let's ask how dayfly makes its hours

and oak what it feels to be in the ground. Let's talk

to the devil himself, licking the tepid blooms

of the hibiscus like the venomous snake.

2.

Turpentine sweated us through summer

slaking our skin trees bled and burned

white faces in the forest a sea of pine stumps

the fire the spring that's to say

the ground water to drink when found

the hands the feet within the heart

an ailing bird over the sand how low

it flew a song blown through air

we want to remember song

we want to sing and dream sweet things.

3.

Sing as grandfather heron soars—

franhnkh, franhnkh—the first heart morning makes,

Sing fantasia, el largarto,

and the waters dance, all hours of the spring.

4.

Plovers huddle on the last piece of land.

I say, come onto the waters,

and when sunset embers,

we'll turn back

hours—evil and great—

and in Florida's most quiet,

sssssss, follow breathmaker

come short of paradise.

City by the Sea

I saw the sun fit gold cubes on the stirred sea,
on the backs of dolphin, the wood-slatted pier,
oyster shacks and fresh signs: Bay Seafood
Back Bayou Bakery. Tide rose. Tide pulled
on its table of minutes and fell:
early high, low; late high and low.
Water dragged by the wrecked pilings
of the railroad from Fernandina Beach,
cleaning the mud flats, the golden mud
crowded with ibis, crabs, each
with its shrieks and dark laughter
heard that once, one time only.
I remembered shade, I felt heat,
I heard the ticking, lisping tide
that brings red drum, trout, and mullet
to feed at the shore's grass cuff.
How to explain how it entered me:
more than the sea but sea of its own sea,
more than the low pale light in sawgrasses
and the long light on the sea, but light
of its own light. Heron's heron. Egret. And gull
in the salt air looking back over its wing
and shoulder, as if it knew it
was leaving behind everything. Day late.
Lights flicking on. Voices then
like skimmers atop the bays,
just below hearing—a tone of pleasure,
a sentence shape of desolation.

Was there an omen?
the turpentine factories,
boats rotting on shoals,
the day-glow X on a shell
and stink of the dead turtle?
Oh, I began thinking of horseshoe crabs
massing on Scale Key; from a distance
they looked like hundreds of helmets,
gold helmets, and turned over
by the waves, they bubbled at the mouth
as if too enraged to speak.
There was no oil yet in the grass;
crossing breezes made crosshatch
on the gold-tented water. Then
I couldn't stop thinking of the crabs—
of omens. The air smelled only
of brine and oyster shells: not oil, not yet
the underwater plumes, tar creatures
swelling, cored of bone, nearing.

Labyrinthine City

An eagle chased the falling
in case the creature drop a feast of sinew and pulverable bone.

Blue-golden surface rushing up,
no branches breaking with honey petals

to soften the blow. No more cunning this day,

this world Icarian.
                        For the moment everything
stopped caring, and those that could flew on.

~ ~

A partridge laughed, secretive in his ground bower,
as the father fathered the drowned arms and head.

Were not other boys cast from heights,
made birds?

                        Horned crab, ant, and the mole soon
dig through the hillock covered with flowers.

Rain ravel in the dry loam. To walk there
would be to sense loftiness brought under.

~ ~ ~

I saw your labyrinth as I rose, my head in spirals.
How could man trick from stone a river's running waves
flowing back to a blind source, then toward open sea?
Once started, how could there be a way back?
Winds roared as I flew, like the roar in my veins.
I breasted upward with the glittering rocking honeyed
air, my lonely impulse for ascent come from you.
I soared. And you must have felt—beyond your
fright for me—the splendor above—an open dome
you may as well yourself have flown to
with your own instrument of wood, wax, and feather.
Then as it came apart I was the ideal
falcon, earth the falconer spiraled to. Or I was an ant
in a triton shell tied to a linen thread
following sweet vapor in the chambers
to its source. The mind perpetually meanders
till eyes are shut, nothing, I thought,
bringing back or revivifying. Yet here we still are—
art and invention riding a fabled wing span,
out of nature, human in failure, telling of
son tied to father, father to son, telling of what is past,
the riddles we come from, and those to come.

Water City

Looking inside the bony plate, perceive
the gray sponge matter that from its depth
breeds without moving.
Colors belong to the surface, reckon
with the wind mounting tidal waves,
clouds' cover, or a ripple of sun.

Underneath, the seeping calculation,
the dark crevasses and only spots of artificial light.
What the mind allows, sucks
without bloat. Unearthly life,
a grouper eats a man whole, the gold
doubloons; something precious,

spontaneous. The gull returns to the sea
food broken down by sharks.
The mind is a sullen scavenger
with the belly and bowels of a god.

Water city, this impure taker
returns so little, a bubble of stupidity,
a salt piece of itself, of what it endures.

Two anthills and a late winter hive gone to fragments. The dirt is acrid, the wax honeyed—so mind makes laws, dividing seasons, scents, light and light's reflections. I have no daughter. Yes, you have a daughter, a voice said. But that is not right. Still, the journey soothes me—No one may come—: low sun, dusk, and charred trees, seeming first to glow as they darken, really are only darkening, as if autumn burned. And if I want it otherwise, O Self, there's beauty in small lies. I say bees lick nectar after dark and bring it to the bough of the honey tree. Royal jelly keeps the larvae from falling from the cells. Broodcomb, honeycomb, bee bread—this is a harmless thought. Yes, once I had a daughter. We lived in two cities. She said to me, there is no twenty on the clock, don't worry. She said, I will tell you the time, I will come to you. She does, the farther I travel away.

Where were you? she asks
Wer bist du I'll say spring
in voices, bird lilt.

—RF

Ornithology

Who else has seen the moment parleying snipe on disappearing
     shoals,
wind frothing at their feet, lift in one loud whirring of wings,
     so the last
are first—a testament time illuminates?
     How many years ago even as now
did another first see morning implement with gold the margins
     of inlet
and marshland, carelessly as the wind blew? Winds, we can tell,
     are jealous
winds and take away the shore, night steals away the gold cup
of day, stars to follow—like a serene flock of birds—and lives
     are taken
in any order, till the last survivors are first, singing themselves
     alone.
Haven't you heard shore birds sing this, in a few notes, and
     known?

Chickadee

For that I cannot know you, I keep you.
For that your reflection in a small mirror
turns your heart tender like mine,
and then you shriek.
For that you let me make small branches
of my fingers for you to climb,
I whistle your sayings.
For that I want a waking bird
in my throat, not colored feather-and-face
but entire. For that the hawk dives on you
and the sky shimmers through your doom.

For that you are caged, I feed you orange oil
seeds and dried papaya. You flute
whether the wire gate is closed or raised.
I clean your cage of offal,
I whistle your sayings
without knowing the meanings—
some tones as delicate as the taste
of poppy, some double-worlded.

What the Dove Sings

The mourning dove
wearing noon's aureole
coos from the rhododendron,
oo-waoh, shadow o-
ver what to do. Oh.
And the sad rhetoric spreads
through suburb and wood.
Those who hear
dove moan love no
querulous warbling more—
the going hence
about which is there no-
thing to do?
From no small rip in fate
the you you never shall be
more will be extracted.
Dove knows the rubric
and starts in, who,
who is next and soon?

How Music Came into the City

From wild, half-peopled hills
I have brought to your streets
sixty-six birds, rare species
of hummingbird and frightened little finch
with their beaks sealed shut
so they would not be heard singing
until I arrived. I sewed them inside
my clothing, simple songs
past hearing for the days
when silent snow mocks stone
and loud voices voice
the wasted breath.
Already can you dream
the rubied merriment
when I open my coat
and unspool the ribbon
from their beaks;
and the heartbreak
when a sole bird falls earthward
as if from a golden tree?
Listen now for the key
of what has been—
a tiny magnitude pouring
myrrh and wind
onto the avenues,
rustle in the undertones.
It will take you back
to the hills and take
the hills away.

I was past the turnstile, a woman about to board a subway, when someone clenched my necklace. The links didn't give, and I was pulled along, my coat and legs an avalanche I let myself be in. If anyone spoke I didn't hear, and whatever glances came my way were knocked down. In a sudden I was left alone. I rubbed my throat and felt for my new hat—straw and a sprig of cherries for spring.

Now and now and now
the air is sweet, even stars
die in that sweetness.

—RF

First City

The mind is a wilderness like Bartram's, razed, cemented over,
     marked by rows
of parked cars and citizenry stones of those less and less well
     remembered.
It is Muir's "glorious forest" and turpentine factories, and
     Audubon's pistol shots.
For mind, like Audubon's, contains birds of every description,
     the pretty one on my sill
with painted crest and impossibly red bill and feasting vultures.

                        The commotion
in so much stillness lured me nearer in my kayak and I waved
     my paddle high
when the vultures circled back for more of the carcass, scattered
     and rotten.
Mind possesses and is possessed by bits of history.
And Arcturus, and the houselights
in cities, when there is no other light, blazing like stars. And
     the human
voice, your laughter in the null moment,
at null o'clock before one last good night.

Lion City

Shi Cheng

Light does not waken the lion,
so deeply still is she, drowned in the valley.
I tried to imagine the eels and carp
nudging her stone flanks, the five gates
to the darkened heart. And then I thought
of the souls who had left
and how the city had borne
the preserved wooden beams and staircases—
her most obstinate desire to keep
what *had been* in one piece. Forgot the noise
of the flood, forgot valley animals running,
as if from beaters in hot bush and rushes.
Soon there was no more wind, rain, or sun.
Lion city lay so still she ceased
to exist. When divers sweep their lamps
through ideograms of bubbles
toward the entrances, the lion-dogs
will still bare their teeth and growl.
Small wonder art outlasts rule.
Lion-mouthed lights drift in the streets,
and milky parts of our night sky
swing out over earth's ruins.
Unnerved by the growing absence
of scents mixed with urine on grass
and bushes, I start an elegy.
Lions fatten on the plains,
We can see all souls that departed

at all given moments. There is plenty,
and then there is no more plenty.

Song of the City at Night

Whatever hid the sun and moon inside a mountain
brought people there to found the night
where a city swans on river water
laving with light each passing wake,
mesmerizing a couple on the riverbrink.
They seem unaware what is myth
or real, taken up, as it were, by a swan's bill
and flown to a milkwater world
where it's possible to drink only the milk
and eat pearls. A gunshot, a siren
interrupts the quiet. Something is thrown
into the river, then the swan is mute.
To sing of this the swan would have to out-swan
itself, Sibelius out-Sibelius Sibelius.

Walled City

Their music was like music in other cities,
sway and pounding, jazz and chorus; their iniquities
no less and no greater when we read minutely
their religious texts. That I might have honey
and dates read one book; the other, that existent
in all things, even non-living things such as stones,
glory was alive and not abstract. There was desire
and sexual pursuit, covetousness, lulls of speech,
oratory, false-smiling, whispering, bigotry.
So shut in, though they had their lives,
they looked for what might drop on them
from the skies. Death could. Hadn't the incorruptible
been changed like to birds and other things?
They set upon the haters of their way of life,
inventors of evil, blood-minded, despicable.
They told them that they knew they could commit
things worthy of death and killed them.
Some avowed loyalty. Avowals of loyalty,
avowals of justice and revenge filled the air
above the place where the ATM blew up, seven dead.

Himalayan

Call for stars and atoms, abyss and rime.
Call avalanche to cover up the climbers left behind.
Let no one any longer see how cold they are.
Sweep off empty cannisters and Mallory's torso,
preserve no more misgivings. Bear these heights alone.
Mind sundown wrestling on the shoulders.
Mind the death zone—air, air, air—and go back down,
then tomorrow like shoeless sheep
leave earth behind with its examples of falling,
what's right and what's wrong
no more than dispersing and building clouds
on the mountain. Make yourself no elegy
but the stone snows swallow then exhume.

Autumn fattened and thinned; I stared at the clock's senseless hands. I let the girl in Publix make change, I looked at my lists of medicines and the bottles on the shelf, but they seemed separate. In the bathroom mirror my face was suddenly antediluvian who was I? I'd be thinking and at the first touch of attention, I'd forget. If I went to the end of the street, would I be at the center of myself? I'd be at the opera house in Vienna. The planes strafed the Strassenbahn.

For a little while I was two persons, old and young, wise and clean, sturdy and bent, generous and dead. They were neck on neck like winter and spring but could do nothing for each other. I'm leaving, I know, each said, a flooding darkness in their eyes, a drawing down of blinds. Afterwards my feelings were the eyes of moths—

They ...
what is the word between eyes
and too little light?

—RF

Everyday City

When fate's hands tore the city in two,
a photographer stood in the middle
of the street and with no right to the view
looked in the bedrooms and toilets.
There was the basic box next to another
box, bristling with mirrors, colored dishes,
that somehow had the power
to make a life seem unique,
rooms in an imaginary encyclopedia
of everyday life, locked in the edges
of photos, on the screen of a video—
here a formica table, there....
Who hasn't relished the idea
of walking without knocking into rooms
that aren't our own, to briefly live
someone else's life, to feel at home
and fascinated with the horsehair couch,
the closets with bed-sheets and smocks,
a grandfather's engraved pocket watch,
its paper-thin initials outlasting him
and us, perhaps. Why had it been left?
Not even the Wunderkammer Olberich
with its unicorn's horn (narwhal tusk),
mermaid's hand, chalices of coconut
and pink-polished conch with gold,
preserved Nile crocodile, lit parrots,
landscapes with sleeping moon, saint's knuckles
in the end is more curious

than the building with empty daylight
of walls and windows torn open
and into which we could pour
our intense feeling for the everyday,
day in and day out, thinking
this is almost what I once was.

Smallwood City

A city of one wood building raised up on stilts
does nothing to hold back the sea but modifies the waves
bays hurricaned dark and light hurricaned
traders reckoning Chokoloskee right where wind
has hung someone's blowing coat someone in a hurry.
By memory by stars stars' debris
by floating transom about to be struck
by boat's prow can we not sense
the patch of calm water near
Smallwood's store, and moor there?

Last City

Cockroaches ignored the winter dawn
lengthening past spring and into summer.
They hid and scarcely saw that we were gone,

but died less frequently from nerve poison
and ruby dust, more and more in nature.
Cockroaches ignored the winter dawn

that froze the buildings. Where spiders spun
their icy webs in icier zephyrs,
they starved and didn't know that we were gone.

Sidewalks heaved, sewers split, bridges came down,
freezing and thawing in long November.
The hard structure of their world in winter dawn

disintegrated, and goose grass, autumn
olive tree, birch, bear, wolf took over
everywhere. The cockroaches were soon gone.

We are like cockroaches of autumn
burrowing more deeply and unaware
in heated cities of the cold dawn
when all we've had will be gone.

Moss City

City down to the last nuance is moss,
straightleaved, twisten, fossilized in travertine,
some that lives on rotting
wood or the sunniest crest in Central Park,
other whose resilience but for a cup of water is stifled.
Mosses don't need to grow flowers
or fruit or wings—angels are or are not here, birds some—
to show continuous creation. They are not degenerate
but remind us of degeneracy.
They are what the imagination needs.
Bellevue, storefronts of diamond cutters,
banks, scripture on placards,
men shouting at each other in voices pure as iron
and tar, museums of modern art,
theatres, tacquerias are side by side,
but moss is what the imagination needs.
With buttermilk, cheap beer, or water
make a slurry. Spores will appear on compacted soil
if acid is high and in deep shade.
Hundreds upon hundreds of versions
and sillouettes will billow forth
in a green cosmos: turrets, hair arrows,
flames and fans
to grapple with nothing it has yet known.

Perpetual City

Mixtures of blue and yellow on winter white
      walls.
pussy willow arranged in a dry vase,
The Book of Beasts,
sundial, desk waterfall, heron
of teak, bill and chest
shaped of one substance: Thus someone
recreates life after life
inside the city. *Yah. Yah. Yah.*
On the paved streets weight thrown
on the ball of the foot, while the other thigh
is lifted. To think how walking
confounded the mechanical engineers,
their extraordinary patience with the clumsy
first robots. Twelvemonth and twelvemonth
      after
with cities put to sleep, icebergs melted to nothing,
they could do everything we could think of,
haunted by our hope and faith and pity
      and hate.
When they came in numbers we recoiled
but remembered the last sleeping place
of Heraclites, Aristotle, and Boneparte
the soup wagons of old wars.
We saw they could smile, their limbs
ready perpetually to do what we no longer
wanted—
sweep the night stars

for changeless meaning, the uncommon in each
breath and step begotten of each breath and step.

Was my mind ever mine to have, my mind given … the floating world … darkness of water, no stars at all, no, no spindrift light, no nearness that in sudden whirlpool doesn't sink and cease to remember.

If I walked to the end of the street would I find myself? Dusk's tarnish. The humble sense of being. Heartbeat from mountains far off … and movement in hydrangeas.

My daughter and son-in-law held my elbows but there was no one in the mirror. I was in eine Garten under hydrangea dirt, I was drowning … gulls a child sobbing, gulls, gulls.

Rode the ship alone, rode the train from Toronto. The mountains weren't near, why should a father be? Memories like snow drowning in black water in the steamer's wake, brother lost in Russian winter.

Why shouldn't snow smother the black water? In the red glow of some evening, somewhere, neon sails.

—RF

NOTE

RF: An Austrian émigrée, Renée Fellner lived through WWII in Vienna and the Tyrol. She rarely spoke of the war until her eighties, when she seemed to know what is lost to silence. Before her language faded completely and she could no longer even see herself in her bedroom mirror, she wrote a handful of what she called her stories. The RF segments in the book are in homage to her invention of herself.

Acknowledgments

Thanks to the editors of the following print journals, online magazines, and anthologies in which some of these poems first appeared, sometimes under different titles.

Academy of American Poets Poem-A-Day: "Circus City" and "Song of the City at Night"

Antaeus: "Water City" (as "The Salt Lesson")

Devouring the Green: "Labyrinthine City" (as "Daedelo")

Gettysburg Review: "City of the Ridiculous," "City with First-Class Funerals," "City by the Sea," and "Impressions of the City"

Great River Review: "City with Rabbit and Crow" (as "The Rabbit and the Crow) and "How Music Came into the City"

Harvard Review: "Impressions of the City at Sunrise"

Kenyon Review: "City Near Paradise" (as "Florida")

Like Light: 25 Years of Poetry and Prose by Bright Hill Poets & Writers (Bright Hill Press, 2017): three interludes as excerpts from "In the Steamer's Wake" ("Evening light rushing back," "I'd loved the ones I Left in Wien," "Was my mind ever mine"), "Smallwood City," "Brandenburg Gate."

Miramar: "Chickadee"

Plume: "Perpetual City," "City Harbor," "Dog City," "First City" (as "Wilderness"), "Mole City," "Moss City," "Last City" (as "Population Zero"), and five interludes as excerpts from "In the Steamer's Wake" ("After I saw my friends dead," "A glimmer sometimes forms as a city," "Autumn fattened and thinned." "I was past the turnstile," "Two anthills and a late winter."

Poetry: "Alias City" and "What the Dove Sings"

Poetry International: "Everyday City," "Rumored City," and "Walled City"

Shenandoah: "Lion City"
Solstice: "Butterfly in the City"
Subtropics: "Ornithology"
The New Republic: "Himalayan"

About the Author

Carol Frost's books include *Honeycomb* (TriQuarterly Books, Northwestern University Press, 2010); *Love & Scorn, New and Selected Poems* (Northwestern University Press, 2000); *Pure* (Northwestern University, 1994); and *The Salt Lesson* (Graywolf Press, 1976).

Her poems have been published in four Pushcart Prize anthologies and in magazines across the country. Some of those publications include *American Poetry Review, Antaeus, The Atlantic, Gettysburg Review, Georgia Review, Harvard Review, Iowa Review, Kenyon Review, Mademoiselle, Massachusetts Review, Michigan Quarterly Review, Missouri Review, Ninth Letter, Ohio Review, The New York Times, New England Review, New Republic, New Letters, North American Review, Northwest Review, Partisan Review, The Paris Review, Ploughshares, Prairie Schooner, Poetry, Poetry International, Poetry NOW, Shenandoah, Solstice, A Magazine of Diverse Voices, Southern Review, Subtropics, Third Coast, TriQuarterly,* and *Virginia Quarterly Review.*

Frost was poetry co-editor with Martha Collins of *Pushcart Prize XXVIII,* and in 2005 she was on the poetry panel of judges for the National Book Awards. She is the recipient of two NEA Fellowships; she directs the Winter With the Writers Festival of the Literary Arts at Rollins College, where she holds the Theodore Bruce and Barbara Lawrence Alfond Chair in English; and in 2019 she was named a chancellor for the Florida State Poets Association.